Stock Market Mindset

The Psychology of Trading Success

DALUXE INC.

Daluxe Inc.

Copyright Page

This book is intended solely for informational and educational purposes. It should not be used as a substitute for professional, financial, or legal advice. The author and

Welcome, future market maestro!

Before we dive into the thrilling roller coaster of stock market psychology, let's take a moment to appreciate where you are. You're holding a book that promises to unravel the mysteries of trading success—not by providing you with a crystal ball but by helping you master your most potent trading tool: your mind.

This book isn't just a guide; it's your GPS through the often-confusing landscape of emotions, biases, and market madness. Whether you're a seasoned trader seeking a mental edge or a newbie still figuring out a candlestick pattern, you're in the right place.

Get ready to laugh, learn, and maybe groan at a few dad jokes. Because here, trading isn't just about numbers—it's about mindset. And you, my friend, are about to level up.

Table of Contents

Chapter 1: Embracing the Trading Mindset

Greetings, courageous reader, and welcome to the thrilling journey of trading psychology! In the intense realm of trading, it's common to think that achievement depends solely on having an ideal strategy, selecting the right stock, or even possessing a crystal ball. However, let's set the record straight from the beginning: it will only matter a little if your mindset is aligned correctly.

In reality, trading involves as much psychological strategy as it does numerical analysis. Every market movement, every price jump or drop, triggers a reaction in our brains. If left unchecked, these reactions can lead us to behave like emotional whirlwinds instead of rational investors. Consider this: how often have you seen a stock climb and felt that irresistible urge to buy, buy, buy? Or watched a market dip and thought, "Maybe I should sell before things worsen?" Trading psychology stands between those knee-jerk impulses and steady, well-thought-out decisions.

Now, it gets even trickier. Our minds can be surprisingly sneaky. They are filled with biases, emotional traps, and tendencies to overreact or underreact at the worst possible moments. This book aims to help you recognize these mental pitfalls for what they are so you can sidestep them with the grace of a seasoned trader.

Why Your Mind Matters as Much as the Market

If you've been in the trading world for more than five minutes, you'll know that stock prices don't just reflect a company's earnings or the latest economic data. Human emotions also influence them: excitement, fear, hope, and good old-fashioned FOMO (Fear of Missing Out). And guess what? Those emotions don't just belong to "the other traders" — they're swirling around in your mind, too.

To truly understand market behavior, you must understand your responses. Why? Because while you can't control the market, you can control how you react to it. And trust me, your reactions make all the difference. Trading with a cool head and a sharp mind helps you stay focused when everyone else is panicking over a market dip or a "once-in-a-lifetime" rally.

What to Expect in This Book

In the pages to come, we'll explore the inner workings of the trading mindset. This isn't just about avoiding common psychological traps in the market; it's about building a rock-solid foundation for success that can withstand the highs, lows, and everything in between. Here's a preview of what we'll cover:

Understanding Biases: We'll uncover the mental quirks that trip up traders, such as confirmation bias, overconfidence, and loss aversion.

Managing Emotions: You'll learn practical strategies for staying calm, whether the market is surging or sinking.

Cultivating Discipline: A robust trading mentality involves not only knowing the necessary actions but also persistently executing them.

Balancing Risk and Reward: We will help you find the right balance between taking informed risks and knowing when to hold back.

Practicing Mindfulness in Trading: Indeed, this is true—meditation in the context of trading. Mastering the art of staying centered can be your greatest asset.

How This Book Can Help You Outwit the Market

Our ultimate goal is simple: by the end of this book, you won't just be trading with a sharper mind; you'll be trading with clarity. You'll learn to identify when emotions or biases are creeping in and have the tools to avoid impulsive decisions. This isn't a book about predicting the market or telling you exactly when to buy or sell. It's about equipping you with the psychological resilience to make smarter decisions, time and time again.

So, please take a deep breath, get comfortable, and let's dive into the art and science of mastering your mind. Welcome to the world of trading psychology—a realm where your greatest asset isn't your portfolio but the clarity of your mind. Ready to begin? Let's get started!

Chapter 2: The Power of Perception

Seeing the Market as It Is

Welcome to the world of perception, where what you see in the market often isn't reality but a colorful interpretation painted by your mind. In trading, seeing the market as it truly is—as opposed to how you *want* it to be—can be the difference between success and "Why did I buy that stock again?" This chapter is about peeling back the layers of cognitive bias to see market trends and signals with clarity, not with rose-colored glasses or fear-tinted ones.

How Cognitive Biases Shape Our Perception of the Market

Think about the last time you watched a stock rally or dip. Were you convinced it would keep going? Could you practically see where it was headed next? That's perception at work. Our brains have a funny way of filtering information to fit our expectations and assumptions.

Cognitive biases are the mental shortcuts we use to process information. While useful for quick decisions, these biases can also lead us astray, especially in the unpredictable trading world.

The two biggest offenders here are *confirmation bias* and the *illusion of control*. These biases can make us cling to information that fits our beliefs, ignore data that doesn't, and ultimately make decisions that feel "right" but might be off.

Recognizing Common Biases

Confirmation Bias

The "I Knew It All Along" Syndrome

Confirmation bias is that little voice in your head saying, "Look, this stock will go up—I just *know* it!" Then, as you search for information, you selectively notice all the positive news, ignoring any red flags that might disagree with your theory. It's our brain's way of seeking comfort and familiarity, but it's dangerous in the market. Imagine driving down a road while only looking at the signs that say, "Great road! Keep going!" while ignoring the ones saying, "Bridge out ahead."

To tackle confirmation bias, try actively looking for information that disagrees with your belief. It may feel uncomfortable, like rooting for the opposing team, but it can save you from costly mistakes.

The Illusion of Control

The illusion of control convinces us we have more influence over events than we do. In trading, it looks like this: you pick a stock, do a ton of research, and feel like you're somehow in charge of its success. You're not. The market is a beast, and no amount of "good feelings" can make a stock perform.

To overcome the illusion of control, acknowledge the market's randomness. Embrace the fact that even the best decisions don't guarantee success. This doesn't mean giving up on research or strategy; it just means remembering that even the best-laid plans are still at the mercy of market whims.

Strategies for Approaching the Market Objectively

Let's get practical. Knowing about these biases is one thing, but how do we actively train ourselves to see the market as it is?

Start with a Blank Slate Every Day

Every morning, approach the market as if you know nothing. Treat each trading day as a new opportunity to assess the facts objectively. This will help you avoid clinging to yesterday's assumptions and keep your mind open to current data.

Use Data as Your Compass, Not Your Hunches

Develop the habit of basing your decisions on data, not gut feelings. Remember, numbers don't have biases, and charts don't have emotions. Use reliable metrics and analyses as your trading guide, and give your gut the day off.

Develop a 'Bias Buster' Routine

When you decide, pause and ask yourself: "Am I seeing what I want to see, or what's there?" Create a checklist for yourself:

- Am I ignoring any negative information?
- Have I checked for different perspectives on this trade?
- Have I considered why this trade might fail?

By taking a few moments to answer these questions, you'll force yourself to examine your choices with a critical eye.

Seek Out Dissenting Opinions

Yes, this sounds painful, but it's effective. Follow a few market analysts or join trading groups that often disagree with your views. It will expose you to alternate perspectives and keep you grounded. It's the financial equivalent of having a friend who always plays devil's advocate— annoying but surprisingly valuable.

Keep an Emotions Journal

An emotions journal can be a game-changer. Write your thoughts, fears, and expectations before and after each trade. This exercise helps you spot patterns in your thinking over time. You'll begin to see how biases influence your decisions and become better equipped to sidestep them.

The Power of Seeing Clearly

The market is a wild ride, full of ups, downs, twists, and turns. To navigate it successfully, you have to be a clear-sighted trader. It is crucial to see the market as it is—as opposed to how you *wish* it were. Perception is mighty but only powerful when rooted in reality, not our biases.

Remember: every trader brings their own "lens" to the table, shaped by past experiences, expectations, and emotions. Your goal is to clean that lens as best as you can. With some practice and self-awareness, you'll spot biases before they take hold and see the market with the clarity that most traders lack.

So, the next time you think, *"I just know this stock is going to soar,"* take a step back. Look at the facts, challenge your assumptions, and keep your perception rooted in reality. Trading success isn't about knowing the future—it's about seeing the present with honesty and accuracy.

Daluxe Inc.

Chapter 3: Mastering the Mental Game

Developing a Resilient Trading Mindset

This chapter explores the creation of mental strength essential for adapting to challenges, recovering from difficulties, and achieving lasting success. Prepare yourself, as cultivating a resilient mindset for trading is a demanding endeavor—it's similar to trekking up a steep mountain while bearing a portfolio on your back.

The Importance of Resilience and Grit in Trading

First, it's essential to recognize that trading is not for the faint of heart. It's a field where you can feel on top one day and be left wondering what went wrong the next. Resilience and grit are the qualities that keep you coming back, learning from your mistakes, and making gradual improvements. Why is this important? Because the market is unpredictable, losses will occur regardless of how solid your strategy is. The critical difference between those who succeed and those who don't isn't the ability to avoid losses—it's the ability to bounce back.

A resilient mindset enables you to tackle trading with the composed assurance of a professional, even when the market seems like an unpredictable roller coaster. Think of resilience as the mental muscle that keeps you steady.

Conversely, grit is the fuel that propels you forward when every instinct suggests that sticking to a regular savings account is better.

How to Bounce Back from Losses Without Letting Them Affect Future Decisions

Let's face it—losses sting. They can lead you to second-guess yourself and your strategy, and the temptation to make impulsive "revenge trades" can be overwhelming. However, resilience means taking losses in stride without letting them cloud your judgment or derail your decision-making process. Here's how to handle losses like a professional:

Acknowledge the Loss, Don't Shun It

Understand that experiencing losses is essential to trading. Every trader, whether a novice or a seasoned professional, encounters these setbacks. View each loss as a chance for growth. Instead of asking, "Why is this happening to me?" concentrate on inquiring, "What insights can I gain from this trade?"

Separate Emotion from Logic

It's easy to feel discouraged after a loss, but try to evaluate each trade independently. Don't allow a single loss to influence your next trade. Develop a mantra like, "One loss does not define my success," and repeat it when feelings of self-doubt creep in.

Resist the Temptation to 'Win It Back' Immediately

This tendency is known as revenge trading and can lead to a slippery slope. Trying to recover a loss with an impulsive trade often leads to more losses. Instead, take a step back, breathe, and reevaluate your strategy with a clear mind.

Focus on the Long Game

Remember that trading is a marathon, not a sprint. Consider each trade a small part of your overall journey. Resilience comes from maintaining awareness of your long-term goals, even when the short-term path is rocky.

Practical Exercises for Cultivating Mental Strength and Staying the Course

Building an ironclad trading mindset takes practice, just like any other skill. Here are some exercises to strengthen your mental game and help you stay on course:

The Post-Trade Reflection Exercise

After each trade, take a few minutes to jot down what went well, what didn't, and how you felt. Consider questions like:

- Did I follow my strategy?
- What could I have done differently?
- What did I learn?

This reflection will help you improve your trading habits and recognize patterns in your thinking. It's akin to keeping a trading journal but with the added benefit of observing your growth over time.

The 'Worst Case' Mindset Practice

An effective way to build resilience is by envisioning the worst-case scenario and mentally preparing for it. Before making a trade, ask yourself, "What's the worst that could happen, and how would I handle it?" This isn't about pessimism; it's about building mental armor. If you're mentally prepared for any outcome, a loss won't feel as devastating because you already anticipated it.

Mindfulness Meditation for Traders

Mindfulness meditation isn't just for yoga retreats; it's also a powerful tool for traders. Daily mindfulness helps you remain calm and focused, even amid market chaos. Just a few minutes a day can make a significant difference. Training yourself to recognize your thoughts and emotions without responding to them will enhance your ability to manage emotional impulses while trading.

Set Small, Achievable Goals

A crucial secret to building resilience is setting small, achievable goals. Start with something simple, like completing five trades without allowing emotions to influence your decisions. When you reach a goal, reward yourself with a small treat (because trading can be hard work!). Celebrating small wins builds confidence, which in turn fosters resilience.

Develop a Pre-Trade Ritual

Establishing a ritual before each trade can help center your mind. This might be as simple as taking three deep breaths, reviewing your strategy, or reminding yourself of your long-term goals.

By applying these approaches, you can develop a strong trading mentality to help you handle the market's fluctuations.

Chapter 4: FOMO and Overtrading

This chapter discusses the powerful emotions of Fear of Missing Out (FOMO) and the pitfalls of overtrading. These feelings can easily cloud your judgment, leading to impulsive decisions that undermine your trading success. By recognizing and confronting these urges, you can develop a disciplined trading strategy that prioritizes long-term gains over short-term thrills. We will provide practical tools and techniques to manage these emotions effectively, enabling you to make sound, informed choices. Embracing this knowledge will enhance your trading experience and empower you to achieve your financial goals confidently.

Understanding Fear of Missing Out (FOMO) in Trading

Fear of Missing Out stems from a human instinct: the worry that others are having a great time without us. In the trading context, it manifests as the overwhelming anxiety that other traders are profiting while we remain on the sidelines. FOMO convinces us that the only way to stay in the game is to constantly buy, sell, and scan for the next big move. Like social media, it exhausts us, second-guessing our choices and occasionally making regrettable trades.

FOMO is particularly tricky because it's rooted in fear and greed. It preys on our desire to maximize gains while minimizing the distress of "what if." When we see stocks surging, our minds instinctively calculate the profits we could have made if we had bought in earlier. That's where the problem lies: rather than focusing on strategy, we start making trades based on what we wish would happen rather than what is likely.

How FOMO Leads to Impulsive Trades

Impulsive trades are the hallmark of FOMO. Picture this: you see a stock climbing, hesitate briefly, but then that ticker keeps rising. Suddenly, without a second thought, you buy in at the peak, convinced you're catching the wave. Minutes later, it dips, leaving you thinking, "Why didn't I wait?" FOMO tricks us into believing every stock or opportunity is a once-in-a-lifetime event. The market is a continuous flow of opportunities, each waiting for the right timing.

Emotional factors rather than analytical reasoning frequently drive impulsive trades. Although trading based on instinct may sound thrilling, it's rarely a sound financial strategy. When you feel that surge of urgency, it's FOMO tugging at you, whispering, "You're missing out!" The secret to success is learning to ignore that voice and adhere to your plan.

Techniques to Avoid Overtrading and Stay Patient

Overtrading is FOMO's trusted companion. Once you've dove into one impulsive trade, it's easy to keep the momentum going, believing that "the next one" will compensate for any current losses. However, overtrading is akin to binge-watching an entire TV series in one sitting—exciting at first, exhausting by the end, and generally unwise.

So, how do you break this cycle of FOMO and overtrading? Here are some effective techniques:

Set a Trade Limit

Determine how many trades you can make in a day or week and stick to it. Once you reach that limit, step away from the trading platform. This simple rule encourages you to evaluate each potential trade more carefully and discourages jumping in without a solid reason.

Create a "Cooling-Off" Period

When you feel the urge to enter a trade based on FOMO, take a five-minute break. Use this time to review your trading plan, check your analysis, or even make coffee. This cooling-off period allows you to breathe and consider whether the trade aligns with your strategy.

Embrace the "What If" Game

Ask yourself, "What if this trade doesn't go as expected?" Visualizing potential losses helps keep your expectations realistic and your emotions grounded. Instead of getting swept up in possible gains, this strategy reminds you of the risks and refocuses your mind on logic.

Practice Patience as a Skill

Think of Patience as a muscle you're strengthening. You're building that muscle each time you resist the impulse to trade. Celebrate small victories like avoiding jumping into a trade with proper research. Over time, these small exercises will turn Patience into a trading superpower.

Creating a Strategy That Keeps FOMO in Check

An effective trading strategy is the remedy for FOMO. With a well-defined plan, you're less likely to be influenced by market chatter or the latest trend. Here's a guide on formulating a strategy that helps you stay focused even when market fluctuations urge you to stray.

Define Entry and Exit Criteria

One of the best defenses against FOMO is knowing precisely what you're looking for in a trade. Clearly define your ideal entry and exit points, and write them down. These criteria allow you to assess each opportunity based on objective factors, reducing the impulse to jump in based on emotion.

Set a "No Trade" Day

Designate one day a week (or month) where you absolutely won't trade. This time will allow you to observe the market without the pressure of participation, strengthening your self-discipline. Watching the market without actively trading helps build confidence that you don't have to participate in every opportunity.

Chapter 5: The Art of Detachment

Trading with Your Head, Not Your Heart

In the world of trading, one of the biggest challenges isn't technical analysis, fancy indicators, or complex charts—it's detachment. The ability to step back and view a stock for what it truly is (and not what you wish it were) is as essential to a trader as patience or resilience. Emotional attachment can cloud your judgment, lead you down impulsive paths, and sometimes even turn your portfolio into a dramatic saga. This chapter focuses on embracing the art of detachment, seeing stocks as assets rather than passions, and learning when to let go.

As a legendary trader (and perhaps a wise therapist) might say, "Love your strategy, not your stocks."

Why Emotional Attachment to Stocks Clouds Judgment

Imagine this: You've done your research, selected a stock that seemed promising, and watched it grow. Perhaps it became "your little star," making you feel like a trading genius. Then, the unthinkable happens—the stock starts to decline. Logic dictates that you should cut your losses, but an emotional voice whispers, "It'll come back; just hold on!" Suddenly, a straightforward trade transforms into a dramatic love story, and you find yourself clinging to that stock as if it were your last hope.

This attachment doesn't merely cloud judgment; it blinds it. You start ignoring warning signs, skipping stop losses, and hanging on to hope. And hope, as wise traders know, isn't a strategy. Emotional attachment leads to "rose-tinted chart syndrome," where every red candle appears less alarming when you're rooting for the stock. This distortion makes objective analysis nearly impossible.

How to See Stocks as Assets, Not Extensions of Yourself

To avoid this emotional pitfall, it's crucial to think of stocks as assets—components of a larger strategy rather than extensions of your identity. Each trade is a part of your investment plan, not a reflection of your self-worth. Here are several ways to maintain detachment:

Remember Why You're Trading

You're here to build wealth, not collect trophies. The stocks you buy are tools to meet your financial goals—not proof of your personal wisdom or foresight. Keeping this purpose in mind helps you stay grounded.

Track Data, Not Drama

Develop a system that focuses on facts and numbers rather than emotions. Basing decisions on data—like earnings reports, market trends, or price-to-earnings ratios—rather than gut feelings will lead to more sound choices. Detachment begins with focusing on what the stock is, not what you wish it to be.

Be Wary of "The One"

If you catch yourself thinking of a stock as "the one" that will change everything, take a step back. It's a stock, not a soulmate. Detachment becomes easier when you remember that every stock is replaceable.

And here's a quote to keep handy: "Stocks don't know you own them." While this may sound blunt, it's important to remember. The market is indifferent to your hopes and dreams, and that's a good thing—it helps keep your focus on rational choices rather than emotional wishes.

Letting Go of "Favorite" Stocks and the Trap of "Revenge Trading"

Every trader has that one stock they can't seem to quit. It's the stock that felt right, seemed destined for greatness, and then, unfortunately, did not perform as expected. However, the art of detachment means letting go—even of your favorites. No stock should hold a special place in your heart, only in your portfolio—and only while it's performing well.

The "Favorite Stock" Dilemma

Holding onto a favorite stock can be both financially and emotionally costly. You may hope for a rebound, wish to validate your original analysis, or believe in a miracle turnaround. However, every stock should be evaluated based on its current performance, not past promises. Detachment is about allowing the numbers—not nostalgia—to guide your decisions.

The Trap of "Revenge Trading"

Another hazard on the path to detachment is known as "revenge trading." This occurs when, after a disappointing loss, you dive back into the same stock or a similar one, determined to "win back" your losses. It's akin to trying to rekindle a bad relationship—risky, often unwise, and fueled more by pride than practical thinking.

Revenge trading stems from a desire to even the score, to feel justified, and to erase the sting of a loss. Unfortunately, it rarely goes as planned, pulling you further from objective trading and deeper into emotional decision-making. To avoid this trap, remember: when you're tempted to "get even" with the market, that the market doesn't know or care. It's not personal; it's just probabilities.

Tips for Mastering the Art of Detachment

Emotional detachment in trading is not a skill you can acquire overnight. It requires practice, a mindset, and ongoing effort to balance strategy with self-awareness. Here are some practical tips to help you let go and embrace the detachment mindset:

Set Clear Entry and Exit Rules: The Non-Negotiables

Establishing straightforward entry and exit rules is akin to creating a "trading prenup." You ensure that emotions won't derail your plans by outlining what will happen if things go awry. Before considering a purchase, set firm criteria for when you'll sell. Write these criteria down, either in stone or in your trading notes, so that when emotions start to influence your decisions—whispering, "Maybe this one will bounce back"—you can remind yourself of the rules.

These predefined parameters serve as impartial "referees" for your trades, guiding your decisions and ensuring you play a disciplined game instead of chasing every fleeting impulse. Additionally, it's challenging to develop an emotional attachment when you treat stocks like scheduled appointments.

Use Stop-Loss Orders: Your Built-In Escape Hatch

Consider stop-loss orders as your trades' "break glass in case of emergency" feature. These automated safeguards allow you to set a price limit at which you'll exit the trade without manually hitting the "sell" button in a moment of panic. Think of it as outsourcing your future emotional breakdown to a handy robot.

Stop-loss orders are beneficial because they don't experience second thoughts or sentimental feelings. They are programmed to cut losses, saving you from clinging to false hope. Once a stock reaches that predetermined threshold, you're out—no deliberation and no convincing yourself that it will turn around—just a quick and clean exit. If only we could set these for our relationships, too, right?

Journaling Your Trades: The Trader's Therapy Session

Keeping a trading journal is like having a personal therapist focused solely on your market moves. Documenting the reasoning behind each trade, your emotional state, and any lessons learned can help you identify patterns, including when you tend to overcommit.

Each entry provides an opportunity for reflection on what went well and what didn't, offering insights into your emotional tendencies. Over time, you'll notice recurring themes. Do you often hold onto specific types of stocks? Are there market conditions that trigger revenge trading? By treating your journal as a "trading confessional," you'll begin to view each trade more objectively, making it easier to part with stocks you're tempted to idolize.

Reflect, Don't React: The Pause That Refreshes

In trading, haste often leads to waste. When a trade doesn't go your way, take a moment to pause and breathe before making your next move. Instead of rushing into a revenge trade to "make back" what you lost, consider taking a few minutes or even a day to analyze the situation. This reflection period can save you from compounding one emotional mistake with another.

During this pause, ask yourself a few key questions: Was this trade part of my plan? If not, what motivated my decision? What can I learn from this outcome? This exercise is akin to taking a deep breath instead of honking at the driver who cut you off. It preserves your sanity and ensures your trades remain grounded in strategy rather than reaction.

Develop a "Trade-It-and-Leave-It" Attitude: Move On After the Trade

One mantra to adopt as a trader is this: "Once the trade is done, let it go." For a reason, the market doesn't have a rearview mirror. Rather than fixating on the outcomes of your trades or wishing you had held onto a winning stock longer, embrace the idea that each trade is simply a chapter in your portfolio's story.

This "trade-it-and-leave-it" mentality means no looking back and dwelling on what could have been. Just as you might delete an ex's number, sometimes the healthiest choice is to cut ties completely. By adopting this attitude, you can approach each new trade with a fresh perspective, free from the weight of past trades.

Treat Trading Like a Numbers Game, Not a Popularity Contest

Here's a little secret: the market doesn't care about you. It's indifferent, immune to charm, and utterly unamused by our dreams of instant wealth. And that's a blessing! Treating each trade as a simple numbers game—an equation of probability rather than a personal investment—you'll find it easier to maintain detachment.

Focus on each trade's odds, risks, and potential rewards without getting sentimental; this will help you approach the market with an analytical mindset. Ask yourself, "What are the probabilities here?" If the odds aren't favorable, don't bother pursuing it. It's all about maintaining that detached, almost scientific mindset—crunching numbers rather than coddling stocks.

Cultivate a Diverse Portfolio: Don't Put All Your Eggs in One Basket

If you're prone to developing strong emotional attachments to your stocks, a diversified portfolio can help prevent you from becoming too attached to any single investment. Think of it as having multiple friends instead of just one best friend. When you diversify, you spread your attention across various investments, avoiding a fixation on one "favorite" stock.

Diversification means that while some stocks may be exciting and thrilling, others are there to provide stability and balance. Balancing your portfolio can protect you from the emotional rollercoaster of concentrating on only one investment.

Daluxe Inc.

Chapter 6: Cognitive Discipline

Welcome to one of the most valuable and challenging skills in trading: cognitive Discipline. Adhering to your trading plan, even when the market seems chaotic, is a cornerstone of successful trading. Cognitive Discipline goes beyond self-control; it involves training your mind to tune out the turmoil and remain steady, regardless of market fluctuations.

The reality is that the market has a will of its own. It can throw tantrums, take unexpected turns, and sometimes ignore logic. A well-defined trading plan is your guiding star, helping you navigate market storms and keeping you grounded when others are panicking.

The Importance of Having a Well-Defined Trading Plan

Think of your trading plan as a carefully crafted roadmap. It outlines where to enter trades, when to exit them, and what actions to take in between. Without it, you become vulnerable to every headline, tweet, and gut feeling—like building a house on quicksand.

A solid trading plan should address essential components such as risk tolerance, target profit margins, and specific criteria for entering or exiting trades. When the market heats up, and everything seems unpredictable, your plan reminds you of the guidelines you established during calmer, more rational moments.

Why Does a Trading Plan Matter So Much?

Because without one, emotions take control. When emotions dominate, discipline often goes out the window. A trading plan prevents you from succumbing to every shiny new opportunity, panic-driven sell-off, and impulsive decision that promises instant returns. It serves as your safety net, your lifeline, and sometimes the only voice of reason in an unreasonable environment.

Remember this trading truism: "The plan you make in peace will save you in chaos." You created that plan for a reason, so honor it when things get turbulent.

Strategies to Maintain Discipline in the Face of Unexpected Market Events

There will be times when sticking to your strategy feels extremely difficult. The market may drop just as you are poised to make a purchase, or your long position could face challenges with every downturn, while the news seems designed to make you question your choices. The key is to stay calm and believe in your strategy. Here are some techniques to help you:

Establish Clear, Realistic Goals

One of the best ways to maintain Discipline is to set clear goals. Ask yourself, "What am I truly aiming for?" Knowing your objectives makes it easier to ignore the noise and stick to your plan. When you have realistic, well-defined goals— such as achieving a specific annual return or limiting losses to a certain percentage—these guideposts remind you of your true path. They help you stay focused, even when the market offers unrealistic detours. Remember, you're not trading for excitement; you're trading to reach a predetermined destination.

Embrace the Power of Patience

Patience is one of the most underrated skills in trading. If you're in a trade and the market moves slower than anticipated, resist the urge to make impulsive changes. Sometimes, the best action is inaction. Patience allows you to endure minor fluctuations without reacting to every dip. As the saying goes, "Good things come to those who wait,"—and in trading, this often means allowing your strategy to unfold without chasing short-term gains.

Limit Your News Consumption

In today's 24/7 news cycle, it's easy to get caught up in daily drama. Many headlines claim to be groundbreaking but are often just noise. Excessive news exposure can overwhelm and distract you from your trading plan, filling you with unnecessary doubts. Instead, be selective about the sources you follow and set specific times to check for market developments rather than letting every alert dictate your actions. This way, you can remain informed without allowing the news to control your trades.

Set Up "If-Then" Scenarios

"If-Then" scenarios act as pre-written scripts for specific market situations. They can help you avoid panic in the face of unexpected events. For instance, you might say, "If the market drops by 5%, then I'll hold steady as long as the fundamentals remain sound," or "If this stock dips below my stop-loss, then I'll exit without regrets." By creating these scenarios in advance, you're better prepared for potential contingencies, reducing the urge to make snap decisions and reinforcing your cognitive Discipline during unforeseen circumstances.

Remind Yourself of Past Wins (and Losses)

Discipline can falter when we need to remember why we established specific rules in the first place. Reflecting on past victories can strengthen your commitment to following your plan while revisiting losses, which highlights the importance of avoiding previous mistakes.

Consider this as a highlight or lowlight reel that keeps you grounded. When the temptation to stray from your plan arises, remind yourself of these experiences to reinforce your Discipline.

Daluxe Inc.

Chapter 7: Developing a Smart Approach to Risk Management

Welcome to the exhilarating realm of risk, where traders face daily financial challenges in pursuing wealth. Trading can be compared to a calculated wager, much like a trip to the casino. However, successful traders do not rely solely on chance; they carefully assess risk against reward, executing each decision precisely. This chapter will explore the psychology behind risk, establish prudent limits, and find the right balance where risk-taking becomes a strategic and profitable endeavor.

Understanding the Psychology of Risk – Why Do Some Traders Love It a Little Too Much?

Risk is inherently exciting. The potential for a significant win, especially in an instant, can be thrilling. For some traders, this excitement can be hard to resist. However, it is crucial to acknowledge the difference between enjoying the game and becoming addicted to the thrill.

The psychology of risk-taking often revolves around one primary factor: reward. Our brains are wired to respond positively to rewards, particularly when uncertainty is involved. The excitement of thinking, "Maybe this trade will double my investment," can feel irresistible, triggering the same dopamine-driven excitement seen in gambling or extreme sports. This innate urge explains why some traders are drawn to high-risk plays—they seek the adrenaline and the thrill of a potential win. However, the reality of trading extends beyond this excitement; it is about managing risk wisely to ensure that wins are sustainable rather than mere strokes of luck.

Recognizing When Risk Turns into Recklessness

When risk crosses the line into recklessness, it's essential to stop and ask yourself: "Am I following my strategy, or am I just taking chances?" Reckless trading could be, for instance, making impulsive decisions without proper analysis, or increasing your position size significantly when you're on a losing streak. The first step in proper risk management is recognizing that the market isn't a casino. If you're seeking excitement, you could quickly deplete your resources without realizing it. In contrast, successful traders acknowledge the excitement, manage it, and use it to make informed, strategic decisions.

Remember this quote when you're tempted to take excessive risks: "Make wise trades, not hasty ones. Achieving success in trading is a marathon, not a sprint." By managing your excitement and experiencing the thrill of successful risk management, you'll find that steady, thoughtful profits are far more fulfilling than sporadic thrills.

Balancing Risk and Reward by Setting Rational Limits and Using Stop-Loss Orders

Effective risk management relies on a balanced approach. Think of it as a dance—you want to move with the market without letting it lead you off a cliff. It's vital to set rational limits and utilize tools like stop-loss orders to achieve this.

Setting Rational Limits

Rational limits involve deciding in advance how much you are willing to lose on a single trade or even within a single day. This conservative approach can be seen as self-preservation. For instance, if you establish a rule to limit losses to 2% per trade, you protect yourself from the gut-wrenching pain of losing a substantial portion of your portfolio all at once. This sense of control and security is crucial in the trading world.

By setting these limits, you create a safeguard, reminding yourself that, while the market may tempt you with promises of high returns, your top priority should be protecting your capital. Ask yourself, "How much am I genuinely willing to risk?" Ensure your answer is honest, practical, and aligned with your long-term trading goals.

Using Stop-Loss Orders

Stop-loss orders are the unsung heroes of risk management. Think of them as the reliable eject button in your trading cockpit. A stop-loss automatically closes your position if the market moves against you by a predetermined amount, helping you contain losses before they spiral out of control.

A stop-loss is your way of telling the market, "You're not taking any more of my money." It establishes a pre-set boundary to protect you from emotional responses like panic, frustration, or desperation. Setting a stop-loss also acknowledges that, while you may have confidence in a trade, anything can happen, and having a safety net is always prudent. This reassurance can boost your confidence and keep you focused on your long-term goals.

One important tip for success with stop-loss orders is incorporating them into every trade, not just the risky ones. Discipline is crucial in risk management; stop-loss orders help you maintain that discipline. They regulate your emotions and prevent losses that could lead to impulsive "revenge" trades.

Identifying Your Personal Risk Tolerance

Determining your comfort with risk is similar to figuring out how much heat you can tolerate on a chili scale. Some investors can easily withstand the market equivalent of a ghost pepper, while others might feel stressed with just a hint of black pepper. Recognizing your position on this "risk tolerance" scale is essential for crafting a trading strategy that lets you rest easy at night, avoiding overly timid or reckless tendencies.

Here's a lighthearted and insightful guide to assist you in assessing your market "risk" tolerance:

Step 1: Reflect on Past Experiences (How Did I Respond to My Last Loss?)

Let's explore your personal experiences. Recall a time when a trade didn't go as expected. Did you swiftly move on, or did it feel like your investments had failed you? Evaluating how you reacted to previous gains and losses can provide critical insight into your risk preference.

The Cool Cucumber

If you remain unfazed when a trade declines and strategically plot your next steps, good news—you likely possess a high-risk tolerance. You probably flourish in turbulent situations where patience and planning keep you steady.

The Rollercoaster Rider

If your feelings fluctuate dramatically with each market shift, your risk tolerance is probably moderate. You can endure some volatility, but drastic changes make you feel uneasy. A balanced strategy may suit you best, offering enough thrill while keeping some safeguards in place.

The Risk-Averse Squirrel

If every market downturn feels like a disaster, you might favor lower-risk tactics. Like a squirrel gathering nuts, you safeguard your assets relentlessly. In this case, conservative options with minimal exposure to market swings could be your optimal strategy.

Step 2: Picture the Worst-Case Scenario and How You'd Handle It

Next, envision a worst-case scenario—such as your favorite stock plummeting by 20% overnight. How would you respond? If your reaction is a calm "That's part of the game," your risk tolerance may be elevated. Conversely, you probably lean towards being cautious if you panic and sell. If your feelings are somewhere in between, you might have a moderate risk tolerance, able to accept some level of risk while preferring a safety net.

This visualization exercise prepares you for the unavoidable losses in trading. By considering a worst-case situation now, you'll be better equipped to make rational decisions later, steering clear of emotional ups and downs.

Step 3: Analyze Your Goals and Financial Situation

Your financial aspirations and personal circumstances significantly affect your risk tolerance. You're likely a more conservative trader if your main priority is preserving wealth and avoiding losses. Conversely, your tolerance may be heightened if you're willing to take calculated risks for greater rewards. Think about how these questions resonate with you:

1. Is this money crucial, or am I comfortable losing some of it?
2. Am I trading for short-term gains or long-term accumulation?
3. How will this trading approach impact my overall financial objectives?

Individuals with a long-term investment perspective may handle short-term fluctuations better and take on more risk. In contrast, those with shorter timelines or immediate cash needs may find it wiser to stick to lower-risk approaches.

Step 4: Set a Trading Budget That Matches Your Comfort Level

An essential part of assessing your risk tolerance is defining a trading budget—an amount you can afford to lose without disrupting your daily life. Think of this as the "sleep factor" test: if losing this amount would disturb your sleep, then you're investing too much.

For those with a high tolerance, this budget might constitute a more significant portion of their portfolio, while those with a low tolerance should only allocate a small fraction. The aim is to establish a budget that allows you to trade without stressing over every dollar, enabling you to pursue gains without the feeling that a loss is devastating.

Step 5: Try Out Paper Trading

If you need more clarification on your risk tolerance, consider trying paper trading to practice without any financial exposure. This method is akin to a practice run with simulated money, allowing you to buy and sell stocks in real time without risking actual capital. Use this opportunity to observe how you react to potential losses and assess whether your risk tolerance shifts when managing real funds. It's an excellent way to explore your instincts and evaluate different strategies without the pressure of financial repercussions.

Recognizing the Signals of "Too Much Risk"

Even after you've done all the exercises, life in the market will reveal more about your tolerance. Here are a few signs you're straying too far from your comfort zone:

1. Loss of Sleep: If you're lying awake over trades, chances are you've overstepped your tolerance. It might be time to scale back or adjust your strategy.
2. Constant Checking: Are you refreshing your trading app every ten minutes? That's a sign you're overly anxious about your investments. This continuous checking can lead to impulse decisions, which are almost always counterproductive.
3. Frequent Panic Sells: If you regularly hit the "sell" button to "feel safe" again, it's a red flag that you're trading outside your comfort zone. Find a level where you can hold on without Panic.

The Takeaway: Embrace Your Unique Risk Profile

In trading, one size doesn't fit all, and that's the beauty of it! Embrace your risk tolerance—a powerful part of building a strategy that keeps you grounded and in the game. By identifying where you stand on the risk spectrum, you're already miles ahead in designing a personalized approach that won't push you into stress-induced trades or sleepless nights.

As the saying goes: "Know thyself and know thy trades."

Chapter 8: Confirmation Bias and Selective Thinking

You've researched a stock and are convinced it will rise significantly. Suddenly, it feels as though every information you encounter supports your prediction. It's as if the universe is giving you a reassuring pat on the back, saying, "You're a genius!" But is that truly the case? Or is your mind falling victim to a common psychological trick known as confirmation bias? This chapter will explore how these psychological tendencies can undermine your trading decisions and, more importantly, how you can outsmart them.

The Invisible Puppet Master: How Confirmation Bias Shapes Your Decisions

Confirmation bias is like a sneaky puppet master manipulating your decision-making process. It's the tendency to favor information confirming your beliefs while dismissing anything contradicting them. In trading, this might look like the following:

You're optimistic about a stock, so you read only positive analyst reports and ignore the negative ones.

You notice a single green day in a sea of red and declare it a "rebound."

A social media post aligns with your thesis, making it feel like divine validation.

Why do we fall for this? Because it feels good! Who likes being wrong? However, in trading, this bias can be dangerous. By focusing solely on evidence that supports your beliefs, you create an echo chamber that closes your eyes to risks and alternative outcomes. This is a red flag that should always be on your radar.

Imagine you're fully invested in a tech stock, convinced it will soar after the following earnings report. You scour the internet for articles promoting the company's potential but must pay attention to warning signs like rising costs or declining market share. When the stock crashes, it's not just your portfolio that suffers; it's your pride, too.

Tunnel Vision: The Cost of Selective Thinking

Selective thinking is closely related to confirmation bias. It occurs when we fixate on a specific detail and ignore the broader context. While this may work for photographers, it can spell disaster in trading.

For example, you might focus only on a stock's high volume, assuming it indicates strong investor interest while overlooking that the price is falling. Selective thinking tricks us into seeing only what we want to see, leading to decisions based on incomplete—or worse, misleading—information.

The Domino Effect of Selective Thinking

Selective thinking doesn't just lead to poor trades; it sets off a chain reaction:

- Overconfidence: You believe your thesis is infallible because you've "done your research" (read: cherry-picked information).
- Increased Risk: Feeling invincible, you allocate more capital than you should.

- Emotional Turmoil: When things go wrong, the emotional toll is even more significant because you've ignored the warning signs.

How to Spot Biases Before They Derail Your Trades

Recognizing when they occur is the first step to overcoming confirmation bias and selective thinking. Here are some red flags to watch for:

Avoiding Opposing Opinions: If you're skipping bearish reports or dismissing negative feedback, your bias radar should be highly alert.

Feeling Overconfident: If you are confident that a trade will work out, pause and ask yourself, "What am I missing?"

Rationalizing Poor Signals: If you say, "The market doesn't understand this stock as I do," it's time for a reality check.

Challenging Your Assumptions: The Antidote to Bias

The good news is that you can outsmart confirmation bias and selective thinking with straightforward strategies. These are mental exercises to keep your trading mindset sharp and balanced. One of the most effective strategies is challenging your assumptions. This is the antidote to bias.

Play Devil's Advocate

Before you hit the "Buy" button, ask yourself, "What if I'm wrong?" Make a list of possible reasons the trade could fail. This practice forces you to consider alternative perspectives and evaluate the risks more thoroughly.

Seek Out Opposing Views

Look for opinions contradicting your thesis. Follow analysts or traders with different outlooks. You don't have to agree with them, but their perspectives can help you see the complete picture.

Use Data, Not Emotion

Rely on hard facts, not gut feelings. If you're bullish on a stock, compare its performance to its sector. Analyze its earnings, cash flow, and debt. Numbers do not lie—emotions do.

Establish Guidelines for Impartiality

Develop a checklist for every trade that includes bullish and bearish situations criteria. Avoid trading if a stock fails to fulfill all of your criteria. This approach assists in eliminating emotions from your decision-making process.

Analyze Previous Errors

Consider instances where confirmation bias or selective reasoning misled you. Which warning signals did you overlook? What evidence did you place too much importance on? Gaining insights from these errors can assist you in preventing them in the future.

Embracing Openness: The Key to Growth

Overcoming confirmation bias and selective thinking isn't just about improving your trading; it's about growing as an investor. You become more adaptable and less emotionally attached to your trades by remaining open to new information and challenging your assumptions.

Chapter 9: Embracing Patience and Long-Term Thinking

In a market where every ticker flickers like a neon sign urging you to "Act now or miss out," embracing patience can feel like swimming against the current. However, patience isn't just a virtue; it's a trader's superpower. While the market entices you with fast-paced drama, patience calmly suggests, "Wait, there's more." Let's explore how to cultivate this often-overlooked skill and why adopting a long-term perspective can be a game-changer for your portfolio and peace of mind.

Patience: The Trader's Secret Weapon

Patience and trading sound like opposites. After all, the market thrives on action, volatility, and the thrill of the next big trade. Yet, the most successful traders aren't those constantly clicking "Buy" or "Sell." They are the ones who sit back, analyze, and wait for the right moment—like financial Jedi.

The key is understanding that the market rewards thoughtful timing, not knee-jerk reactions. Impulsive trades often lead to regret, while patient decisions are rooted in strategy and foresight. Think of it this way: a lion doesn't chase every gazelle. It waits for the perfect opportunity and pounces with precision. Be the lion of your trading jungle.

Techniques for Cultivating Patience

Patience isn't something we're born with; it's a skill that takes practice. Here are some techniques to help you build your patience muscle, one trade at a time:

Practice the 30-Minute Rule

When you feel the urge to make a trade, stop. Set a timer for 30 minutes and use that time to review your trading plan. Ask yourself:

- Does this trade align with my strategy?
- Am I reacting to news or acting on analysis?
- Is this a fear-of-missing-out (FOMO) moment?

By the time the timer buzzes, you'll often realize the trade wasn't as urgent as it seemed.

Focus on the Process, Not the Outcome

Patience grows when you shift your mindset from "I need to make money now" to "I need to stick to my strategy." Celebrate small wins, like following your rules or avoiding a bad trade. Each disciplined decision reinforces your patience.

Meditate

Trading can be stressful, and meditation can help you stay calm amidst market noise. Even five minutes a day of focusing on your breath can improve your ability to pause and reflect before making decisions. Think of it as training your brain to trade in a Zen-like state.

Turn Off the Ticker

Constantly watching the market can lead to impulsive actions. Take a break from the screens. Go for a walk, read a book, or do anything that reminds you there's life outside the stock market. The market will still be there when you return—promise.

Set Clear Entry and Exit Points

Pre-defining your entry and exit points helps eliminate emotional decision-making. When you know your plan, you're less likely to act on whims and more likely to stick to your strategy.

How to Shift Your Mindset to Long-Term Thinking

Adopting a long-term mindset is similar to learning to enjoy kale smoothies. It may not seem exciting, it doesn't provide immediate satisfaction, and it certainly isn't what your brain craves, quick rewards, or desires. However, like those smoothies, embracing long-term thinking ultimately pays off—helping you build a healthier portfolio and perhaps a bit more peace of mind. Let's break down the steps to transition from someone who seeks immediate gratification to becoming a master of patience as smoothly as possible.

Define Your "Big Why"

Trading without a long-term goal is like driving without a destination. It's fun to hit the gas and feel the wind in your hair, but eventually, you'll run out of fuel with nothing to show for it. Start by asking yourself:

- Why am I trading?
- What does success look like for me?

Are you building a retirement fund, saving for your children's education, or aiming for that dream yacht named "Compound Queen"? Your "why" serves as your guiding star. Please write it down, stick it on your monitor, or keep it somewhere visible. Every time the market tempts you to act impulsively, remind yourself of your "why." It's easier to resist short-term thrills when focused on long-term fulfillment.

Stop Trying to Outsmart the Market

It's impossible to outsmart the market consistently. Even the most skilled analysts on Wall Street cannot predict every fluctuation. So, what's the point of trying? Embracing a long-term perspective means releasing the unrealistic belief that you can perfectly time every market peak or avoid every downturn.

Instead, focus on staying in the market rather than trying to time it. Historically, markets reward those who remain invested during both good times and bad. Think of it as planting a tree: you don't dig it up every week to see if it's growing. You let it flourish over the years, nurturing it with patience and discipline.

Reframe Your Thinking About Volatility

Volatility is the market's way of reminding us that it is alive and dynamic. Instead of viewing volatility as your enemy, think of it as an over-enthusiastic puppy—unpredictable but manageable.

When the market declines, your immediate impulse may scream, "SELL EVERYTHING!" However, your long-term mindset should calmly respond, "This is just a temporary dip. It's a buying opportunity." Here's how to reframe your thinking about volatility:

- Look at the Bigger Picture: Pull up a long-term chart of the S&P 500. Notice how it has trended upward over the decades despite numerous short-term setbacks.
- Focus on Fundamentals: Strong companies weather storms. If you've invested in solid businesses, trust their ability to recover.

Remember, volatility is just noise. Long-term investors don't flinch; they strategize.

Celebrate Small Wins Along the Journey

Long-term thinking doesn't mean ignoring the present. It involves finding joy in the small milestones that align with your strategy. Did you resist the urge to panic-sell during a dip? Celebrate that! Did you stick to your investment plan instead of chasing the latest meme stock? Give yourself a high five!

These small victories reinforce positive habits. Over time, they will snowball into a disciplined approach that becomes second nature. By celebrating progress, you're training your brain to value patience over impulsivity.

Automate Your Investments

Humans are notoriously bad at sticking to plans, especially when emotions are involved. Automating your investments is one of the smartest moves you can make. Automation removes the temptation to meddle and ensures you're consistently investing, regardless of market conditions.

Approaches such as dollar-cost averaging (DCA) simplify this process. With DCA, you consistently invest a set amount over time, independent of market fluctuations. This method helps mitigate volatility and encourages a long-term perspective. It's akin to having a financial autopilot—steady, reliable, and unaffected by emotional ups and downs.

Seek Out Long-Term Role Models

Every field has its heroes, and investing is no exception. Warren Buffett, often called the Oracle of Omaha, has built an empire by sticking to long-term principles. Read about investors who have thrived by being patient, disciplined, and focused on the future.

Their stories are not only inspiring but also instructive. Learn how they navigated market crashes, resisted fads, and stayed the course. Channel your inner Buffett and remind yourself that slow and steady wins the race.

Turn Down the Noise

The modern investor's greatest challenge is information overload. Between news alerts, social media, and 24/7 financial channels, it's easy to become overwhelmed by the chaos. However, most of that noise doesn't matter.

Mute the distractions. Unfollow the doom-and-gloom commentators. Instead, focus on the metrics and strategies that align with your long-term goals. Less noise equals fewer impulsive decisions—and more room for calm, calculated moves.

Visualize Future Success

When the urge to chase quick wins arises, pause and picture your future self. Imagine opening your portfolio in 10 or 20 years and witnessing the compounded growth. Visualizing your success can strengthen your commitment to a long-term investment strategy and inspire patience as you pursue your financial goals.

Chapter 10: Mindfulness and the Art of Staying Focused in High-Stakes Trading

Imagine a high-stakes trading day, where the markets are volatile, your screen displays a chaotic array of colors, and your heart races like a caffeinated squirrel. Welcome to the world of high-stakes trading, where emotions can run high, and decision-making is often clouded by stress. But what if there were a way to remain calm, focused, and grounded amidst the chaos? Enter mindfulness—your secret weapon for transforming anxiety into clarity and impulsivity into precision.

The Mindful Trader: Why Staying Present Matters

Mindfulness is more than just sitting cross-legged and chanting "om." It's the practice of being fully present, aware, and accepting of the moment—without allowing your thoughts to spiral into panic or overanalysis. For traders, this means focusing on the trade rather than worrying about the missed opportunity or the market crash you fear.

When mindful, you respond thoughtfully and don't just react to the market. This shift from autopilot to deliberate action can be the difference between making a calculated move and falling into an emotional mistake. After all, the market won't slow down for you, but mindfulness can help you find calm in the storm.

Techniques for Mindfulness in Trading

The Power of the Pause

Before hitting "Buy" or "Sell," take a moment to pause. Breathe deeply and ask yourself:

- Am I reacting emotionally, or am I acting on a strategy?
- Does this align with my trading plan?

This pause creates clarity, allowing you to reassess your motives and make deliberate choices. Think of it as hitting the mental "refresh" button.

Breathe Like a Yogi

Breathing exercises aren't just for yoga enthusiasts—they are vital for traders. Deep, intentional breathing lowers your heart rate, reduces stress hormones, and keeps your mind clear. Try this technique:

- Inhale for 4 seconds
- Hold for 4 seconds
- Exhale for 6 seconds

Repeat this process multiple times, and your tension dissipates like butter melting on a heated pan.

Practice Single-Tasking

Multitasking is the enemy of mindfulness. Analyzing charts, checking news feeds, and sipping coffee all at once dilutes your focus. Instead, concentrate on one task at a time. Whether researching a stock or reviewing your strategy, give it your full attention. The market might be chaotic, but your mind doesn't have to be.

Stress Management During Market Fluctuations

Market fluctuations can feel like a roller coaster ride without a seatbelt. However, instead of screaming through the experience, mindfulness helps you manage stress and maintain stability.

Acknowledge the Stress

Ignoring your stress doesn't work; it only bottles it up for a more enormous explosion later. Acknowledge your stress by saying, "Yes, this is overwhelming, but I'm in control." Naming your emotions can help reduce their hold on you.

Stick to Your Plan

When stress peaks, abandoning your strategy for impulsive decisions is easy. Resist that urge! Trust your trading plan—it's your lifeline in turbulent times. Mindfulness helps you adhere to the plan by keeping you grounded in logic rather than emotion.

Focus on What You Can Control

While you can't control market movements, you can control your reactions. Shift your focus to things within your power:

- Setting stop-loss orders
- Reassessing your risk
- Simply stepping away from the screen for a moment

Daily Mindfulness Practices for Traders

Mindfulness isn't just a tool for emergencies; it's a daily habit that can transform your trading mindset. Here's how to incorporate mindfulness into your routine:

Start Your Day with Intention

Before plunging into the market, take a few moments to set an intention for the day. Ask yourself:

- What's my primary focus today?
- How will I respond to challenges calmly and strategically?

This mental warm-up sets the tone for a mindful trading day.

Schedule Breaks

The market may operate 24/7, but you are not a robot. Schedule regular breaks to step away, stretch, and reset. Even a five-minute walk can refresh your mind and improve your focus.

Reflect on Your Day

At the end of each trading day, take time to reflect. What went well? What could you improve? Mindfulness isn't about perfection; it's about awareness and growth. Journaling your thoughts can help you identify patterns and refine your approach.

The Long-Term Benefits of Mindfulness in Trading

Mindfulness isn't a quick fix; it's a mindset shift that pays dividends over time. Traders who embrace mindfulness report:

- Improved Decision-Making: A more explicit focus leads to better choices and fewer regrets.
- Reduced Stress: Calm traders make calmer trades, creating a cycle of emotional stability.
- Greater Resilience: Mindfulness helps you bounce back from losses with grace rather than frustration.

As you practice mindfulness, trading becomes less about reacting to the market and more about navigating it confidently.

Conclusion: Building Your Trading Edge with Psychology

Well done on arriving at the concluding chapter of this mental training course we refer to as *Stock Market Mindset: The Psychology of Trading Success.* At this point, you have evolved from simply being a trader into a highly refined entity of mental strength, strategic planning, and—if we may say—serene composure. Let's review our journey together. We are excited about your future in the market.

Your Psychological Toolbox: The Greatest Asset You Own

The previous chapters delved into the inner workings of a trader's mind—the good, the bad, and even the irrational. We've equipped you with tools to navigate the chaos of the markets while maintaining your composure. Here's a quick recap of the psychological weapons now at your disposal:

- Patience: You've learned to wait for opportunities rather than chasing after every shiny stock.
- Resilience: Losses no longer feel like the end of the world; they are lessons, not life sentences.

- Objectivity: You can step outside your biases and view the market as it is, not as you wish it to be.
- Mindfulness: From breathing exercises to pausing before impulsive trades, you've embraced the art of staying present.
- Discipline: Your trading plan has become your trusted companion, and you've committed to following it—no matter how tempting the market's siren song might be.

The Key to Success: Practice, Practice, Practice

Just as Trading is a skill, so is psychology; it requires practice. You can't simply read about patience and expect to become the Dalai Lama of Wall Street overnight. So, how do you ensure these principles take root?

- Integrate These Strategies Daily: Consistency is vital, whether journaling your trades, reflecting on your emotions, or taking a mindful pause before making significant decisions.

- Learn From Every Trade: Wins and losses provide growth opportunities. Review them with curiosity rather than judgment.
- Celebrate Progress: You may not have executed every trade perfectly this week, but if you resisted impulsive moves or stuck to your plan, that's a win worth celebrating.

A Final Call to Action: Master Your Mind, Master the Market

While the markets are unpredictable, your mindset doesn't have to be. You are setting yourself apart from other traders by prioritizing psychological strength alongside strategy. Most traders chase the latest hot stock tip or technical indicator, but you're playing the long game.

Remember, your mind is your most valuable asset. Treat it well. Keep it sharp. Feed it knowledge, discipline, and self-awareness. When the market throws you a curveball—and it will—you'll be ready, not rattled.

So, what's next? Take what you've learned here and apply it. Test it. Refine it. The journey to trading success is not a sprint; it's a marathon. The more you invest in mastering your psychology, the better prepared you'll be to thrive in the ever-changing landscape of the markets.

Parting Words: Keep Growing, Keep Trading

Remember that success in Trading isn't about being perfect; it's about being adaptable. The market rewards those who can evolve, remain disciplined, and manage their emotions. You've got this.

Now, trade wisely, and may your portfolio grow as robustly as your mindset. And don't forget to take a break now and then to enjoy the ride—after all, even traders deserve a coffee break or two.

Good luck, and may your trades always trend in the right direction!

Dear Reader,

Congratulations on making it to the end! You've journeyed through the highs and lows of trading psychology, explored the depths of your decision-making, and hopefully emerged as a wiser, more self-aware investor. You've equipped yourself with strategies to tame FOMO, embrace patience, and keep cognitive biases at bay.

This is merely the start of your journey, not the conclusion. Achieving success in trading is a long-term effort, not a quick race, and honing your mindset is essential to remaining competitive. Keep in mind that the market is not your adversary—it's your ally in development.

Consider leaving a review if this book made you laugh, think, or facepalm at least once. Your feedback helps other readers discover this guide and inspires me to write more.

Thank you for choosing "Stock Market Mindset" as your trading companion. Now, trade with confidence, clarity, and just the right amount of humor. May your mindset be strong, your trades be steady, and your profits be plentiful.

Happy trading,

www.ingramcontent.com/pod-product-compliance
Lightning Source LLC
Chambersburg PA
CBHW071522220526
45472CB00003B/1116